"The Teachings of Miss Ellie Ruth"

{A novel for mature minds}

By

Tj Baker

ISBN: 0-7596-5786-6

This book is printed on acid free paper.

1stBooks - rev. 5/22/02

Before I read this book I had almost convinced myself that this was not my type of story. I've read my share of books by black women who portray black men in a negative or stereotypical fashion (sometimes justified). Reading this book reminded me of summers with my grandfather, uncles and other positive role models.

As an online magazine editor, I've gone out of my way to make sure that my magazine has relevant content for women. It was nice to read a book where the "brothers" added value to the lives of others.

Tj Baker tells the stories of men and women whose voices are missing, not because they don't want to speak, but because they don't get heard. That alone made it worth my time.

Gary Johnson
Founder, Black Men In America.com
www.blackmeninamerica.com

Tj Baker enjoys Vanilla Bean coffee and wearing
sexy pajamas.

Acclaim for
Tj Baker

"The Teachings of Miss Ellie Ruth"

Carl Booker – CEO the Juice Magazine **
www.thejuiceonline.com
Ms. Baker is a major contender in the blossoming genre of southern urban storytellers.

Tameshia S. Collins - Texas Southern University staff
"Although, I did not spend the majority of my life growing up on a farm, I enjoy reading novels that trigger reflections upon that time in the country. Reading "The Teaching's of Miss Ellie Ruth" gave me an opportunity to think back and appreciate the times that, I was there and the fun that I had.

Derrick Woods – Boss Productions **
bossproductions@aol.com
Well written, Houston's hottest new talent!

Tj Baker's—Acknowledgments

My son, Keith Douglas Baker II.
Boss productions—Mr. Derrick Woods
My publicist—Mrs. Jill Haynard and staff
My wonderful opinion and spell check friend—
Mrs. Evelyn Rivera
To my family and few friends
A special thanks to a person that helped straighten out my life
Mr. Cecil W. Bentley
A special thanks to Renée W. Spivey of E-Taskmaster, Inc.
Your editing help was invaluable.

Houston—Downtown Public Library—Research Department;
Thanks for finding the words "Lord Don't Move My
Mountain"
Sam Houston State and Texas Southern University
Phi Beta Sigma and Zeta Phi Beta
To the periodicals and writers group that added me to their list.
Voices from the Gap; Celebration of Women Writers; Black
Texas; The Juice Magazine; Our Texas and so many more.
To the Republican Party!

Last but not least
To me—finally a published novelist

Tj Baker

In the 1940s a female was considered to be a woman at the age of thirteen. Ellie is twelve years old and is itching for that big day. Will turning thirteen make her mature? According to her Aunt Effie, *"surviving your mistakes makes one's identity."* Ellie will soon find out that she has a long road ahead of her.

Ellie and her friends discover that maturity is not an easy lesson to learn, especially when you're dealing with hypocrites, Christians, sex, racism, molestation, prejudice, murder and the church.

As you read this story you may find yourself being sympathetic to Ellie and her friends. Perhaps you can identify with their journey. Perhaps you experienced similar events in your past. If Ellie's story doesn't impress or shock you, then get ready for more scandal and intrigue in the follow-up to this novel coming soon to a bookstore near you.

<u>DEDICATION</u>

I DEDICATE THIS BOOK TO GOD.

Proverbs 3:6

In all thy ways acknowledge him, and he shall direct thy paths.

Introduction

Around sunset you can count on two things:

(1) O'l Rufus, the farm rooster crowing up a storm to get every living creature stirring for another day.
(2) Grandma Samford, singing in the kitchen "Lord Don't Move That Mountain"

LORD DON'T MOVE THAT MOUNTAIN

Now Lord don't move that mountain
but give me the strength to climb
and Lord
don't take away my stumbling blocks
but lead me all around
(repeat stanza)
Lord, I don't bother nobody
I tried to treat everybody the same
but every time, I turned my back
they scandalize my name

But Oh Master!

Lord don't move that mountain
but give me the strength to climb
and Lord
don't take away my stumbling blocks
but lead me all around
Now when my folks were slaving
There were things they would try to do
Lord don't touch them
for within their hearts

make them give their lives to you

But Oh Master!

Don't move that mountain
but give me the strength to climb
and Lord
don't take away my stumbling blocks
but lead me all around

___Birds and the Bees___

"Son-of-A-Biscuit Eater! Ellie, Ellie." Grandpa Samford yelled.

"Yes-Sir" from the corner of the barn, Ellie answered.

"Come here and help your grandpa, this doggone tractor done clunked out on me again."

Ellie gave a light giggle as she approached him. "How come you won't buy a new one," she asked. He pats the tractor. "Oh Ellie, it still has a few good years and since you're here well— you keep it running." He winked at her. "Tell me Miss Mechanic," he continued, "What's wrong with it now?"

Ellie let out a sigh, "Mm" as she came closer to the tractor and opened the hood. "Oh I see, hand me my tools please." he said.

"Ellie's tools coming up" he said. Reaching toward the top shelf to get her toolbox, continued he talked. "There, what you need out of it?"

"Ellie's voice," coming up from the hood of the tractor engine, "Give me the small wrench and that should do it."

1

"Ellie, are you through collecting those eggs?" Grandma Samford hollered from the back porch. "She's fix'n the tractor," yelled Grandpa Samford.

"In her school clothes!" The grandmother shrieked. "Hold on to your support hose woman the chile ain't getting dirty," yelled Grandpa Samford.

"That's not the point, it's not lady like. Get that chile from under that tractor right now Nathan Samford!" Grandpa Samford, stormed back inside the kitchen.

"She's not under the tractor she's fix'n the engine." But it was too late the stale wind just carried his voice into the air.

"There you are Grandpa, you can crank her up now" said Ellie as she came up from the hood of the engine. Barely, but successfully her Grandpa Samford climbed into the tractor, turned the ignition and behold it started. "Miss Mechanic, you did it again. Thank you, it sounds like a purring kitten. Now I'm already in deep muddy rivers with your grandma. So go on before she really wants to hang me." said her grandfather.

"Yes—Sir." Ellie smiled.

"Ellie don't forget your eggs." He pointed to the basket. She bent down to get her eggs and started back to the house. Sitting the eggs on the counter she stood upright for inspection.

"Let me look at you, now turnaround." Ellie stood there frozen waiting for approval. "How many times have I told you not to do any carpentry or mechanical work in your school clothes?" Her grandma asked.

"I know, but it was minor—this time" said Ellie. Grandmother Samford's face twisted from her granddaughter's answer.

"I don't know what I'm going to do with you," said grandmother.

"How about love me more" said Ellie as she smiled and gave her grandmother a big squeeze and hug.

Hi my name is Miss Ellie Ruth Samford. I live with my grandparents on a farm. My mom left me here or my grandmother wouldn't let me go. Grandma said my mom had the trademark of a gypsy. The last time, I saw my mother, I was three years old they say. That was nine years ago. About two months ago my Aunt Effie moved in with us. She's the oldest of the five daughters on my grandmother's side. That's how I got my name, from their first initials.

Aunt Effie	She lives with us now.
Aunt Lucette	Lives up yonder by the fork of the road. She's a widow and has three sons.

Aunt Lum	Lives in Chicago. My mom's supposed to be up there too.
Grandma Ivory	Has been happily married to Grandpa Samford for thirty-two years. She had one child—my mother and one grandchild. That's me.
Aunt Eula	Died from polio at the age of eleven.

My middle name is Ruth, which was taken from my mother. I don't miss her.

You can't miss something that you don't love—right? There is one question that I don't have to ask, and that is whether or not my grandparents love me very much. Even my Aunt Effie, who is crazy as a fruitcake's, always making me laughs. She's the type of Auntie that every niece should have. She's open and rationalize everything. She says when you rationalize things you get old quick. Prime example she said. "Look at your grandmother." And, I totally believed her until I saw Aunt Effie secretly put some type of black oil on her hair. But her bones are still in good working order. You should see her, she really can cut up on the carpet rug especially when she hears a good beat on the tune box.

We always turn the tune box after dinner. Our living room instantly becomes a small dancing hall. There's grandma sitting down, just clapping her hands and moving her body from side to side as usual. Grandpa, well he tries to do a step or two ending it with a twist. As for me, I guess I'm all right. My skinny legs have a mind of their own and my feet don't know what's left or right. But dancing sho'll is fun. Aunt Effie and I would show our stuff first. She would show me the past old dance steps and I would show her the present new dance steps. It's a good thing that Aunt Effie picks up real well and can turn it out. Then Grandpa would stand up and say "That ain't nothing—step a side little lady. Come on Effie, I'm your real competition—show me what you got." Then the contest was on. Grandma and I are the judges. One after another they show their dancing talents. Grandpa's knees and feet let him tell it, he taught "The Nicholas Brothers" and Aunt Effie gracefully moved like the one and only "Lena Horn." When the two get through giving their all, grandma and I hover over one another and decide the winner, and as always another tie. On some Saturdays Aunt Lucette and her boys would come over. We form a dance line so that everyone can show off their dance moves. You talking about a hilarious sight to see. Sometimes grandma would get up from her chair and join in the fun. But she might as well sit back down, because she does the same thing when she's sitting. Our dance floor closes around nine pm, so we can put grandma's sitting room furniture back in its place. Aunt Lucette and her boys say their "I bid adieu" and head home. After that grandma would get ready to wash and hot comb my hair for Sunday morning church.

Pastor Coe Caldwell, IV is our leader at Greater "White" Missionary Baptist Church, which was founded by a former slave owner. May God bless his lilly "white" soul. The new rumor is that the officials at the church, are talking, and I repeat just talking about replacing him. Lately he's been preaching about the same two things. {*1*} Adultery—his own experiences and {*2*} Cheating the Lord out of his money—which really means his wallet has not seen a lot of cash lately. I guess you need a lot of money if you're supporting two women. "Now church," Pastor Caldwell would start of by saying, "I preach every Sunday, so you better get right cause the master is coming for his bride, don't know the hour or the day."

"Yeah," a church member shouted from the congregation. Then a church sister leaned forward to another and said, "he better hope in that hour of the day that he's not in the bed doing the nasty with Deacon Chesterfield's wife."

"Amen," yelled the other sister.

"And—Amen to you sister," The pastor shouted. Continuing on went the pastor, "I'm telling you He's coming, and coming soon. Might be tomorrow, might even be tonight, it says that He might come in the middle of the night like a thief while you are asleep. Good Goddy Mighty—so brothers and sisters give big to the Lord. Show him how much you love him. The basket is starting with me first. I'm putting in Five Dollars cause, I love the Lord, yes Jesus, thank you Father." He waved the Five Dollars at us like it was a glorious flag or something! Then he dropped the money in the basket leaned over to the Head Usher and said, "Bring me back my Four Dollars and Seventy-Five cents immediately." He straightens up to the podium and says, "While the basket is being passed around, I wrote something that I'm going to share with my church family, it's a sonata that I wrote and brother Mel Junior is going to play the music for it. It's called 'Misplacing God'."

<u>"Misplacing God"</u>

I have misplaced something
and ever since I misplaced it I've had nothing
but drama and trauma
un-destination of miles and miles as a nightmare walker
I asked God to help me find what I misplaced
for sure my life would turn over for the better.
I know I didn't misplace my lucky rabbit foot or anything like
that
because, I don't believe in it
didn't misplace my zodiac scriptures for I don't read those
don't throw salt behind my back to keep omens away
so what is it?
I haven't done wrong to anybody in general?
Yet ever since, I misplaced what I misplaced
all of my good has turned to evil
and no matter how I communicate
verbally...body language...or words on paper
it just totally comes out wrong
my tears can make a lake and when it comes to frustration
I'm ahead of JOBE!
Talk To Me God...or is it I'm just not listening?
In public, I don't look confused

and even the mirror complimented me this morning {*HA!*}

Whatever I misplaced it's "simple"

God already revealed that one clue to me

and if I sit here and think with a "critical mind"

and not an "open mind" which allows reasons to become good thoughts

If I just sit here, think, pass the flesh, bone and see my soul

that's it

"soul" second clue

let me put this all together

Simple + Soul = Savior

Oh my God, I misplaced you?

How can I misplace you?

I always praise your name up to the highest

I love you and adore you

you are my all

What - my tithes would be my all?

{It is written—Isaiah 6:13—said God}

But yet in it shall be a tenth,

and it shall return, and shall be eaten:

as a teil tree, and as an oak whose substance is in them,

when they cast their leaves: so the holy seed shall be

the substance thereof.

So if I pay my tithes my life will turnover?

When you buy fertilizer don't your crop grow better?

Oh you're sarcastic?

No just honest!

From there, I came out of seclusion

from thoughts, un-puzzled and more Christianity awareness

of never again

Misplacing God

"So brotha's and sista's my daughter, sister Mae Faith Caldwell, is coming down from the choir stand to mesmerize us with one of her songs. And church while she's singing, the collection plate is going to be passed around a second time and don't hold out, but reach in and give out, Amen—Amen!" Rumor has it that Mae Faith had a chance to sing with the big times, but how would it look the pastor's daughter singing the devil's music. "Totally disgraceful," the old women of the church said.

"Ellie, I'm going to the Meyers in another twenty minutes would you like to go?" Grandpa Samford shouted toward upstairs. "Yes—Sir!" Ellie shouted back downstairs. Ellie had this terrible crush on the Meyers son name Israel Robert Meyers. She didn't really know to much about him only that he was eighteen years old, light complexion, about six two in height, wavy hair, hazel eyes, built like a solid tank, all star high school player in football, basketball, baseball and the debate team. That he can cook, has a green thumb, a voice that any woman would love to be serenaded with, his favorite dessert is lemon meringue pie and best of all, he didn't have a girlfriend!

So far he has escaped the shot gun weddings, cause no girl has been able to come close and point that he's the one that pregnated them. Especially sister Mae Faith whose been trying to get him alone since they were in middle school. Rumor has it

11

that he has more sugar in him than a candy cane stick. All because he never entertained sister Mae Faith Caldwell and I don't blame him. Right now he's in transition in switching to another university. And it just so happens that I'm wearing his favorite color-yellow.

"Oh don't we look extra pretty today," said Aunt Effie.

"Tell us what is his name?" asked Aunt Lucette as the two aunts were going upstairs and Ellie was coming down the stairs. "Oh aunties stop teasing," Ellie said.

"Okay, keep your secrets about Israel Meyers, I thought we were friends" laughed Aunt Effie. Ellie froze in her tracks then said, "Aunt Effie, please don't tell grandma, you know how paranoid she has become lately!"

"Yes child, I know, we will talk later. Go on and have some innocent fun before life rob, it from you," said her Aunt Effie.

Before Ellie walked out the door she checked herself one more time in the hallway mirror. Took a deep breath and said, "Okay Israel, here I come." Her grandfather was already waiting for her inside the truck. While they were traveling down the road, Ellie asked her grandfather a question. Shouting "Grandpa, how old are you than Grandma?" Not looking at his granddaughter, but keeping his eyes on the road he said. "Well, I don't know exactly how old she is, see Ellie age doesn't matter {besides, I never ask} we love each other" he ended his phrase. "Well how did you know that she was the one for you?" Ellie asked. Grandpa Samford chuckled and said, "You don't Ellie, it just smack you right dead in the face." Still not looking at her, she continues "A man sometimes deny it, but it grabs him anyway, he can't shake it, so he finally accepts it." "Well does it smack a girl in the face too?" asked Ellie. "Well you know, wait a minute, why?" said Grandpa Samford, while looking at his granddaughter and the road. "I just wanna know," replied Ellie. "Well, Ellie these questions should be answered by your grandmother, since you became a wo-ma," stuttered her grandfather.

"Woman, grandpa a young woman." Ellie laughed.

"Yeah, that word." Her grandfather smiled then his focus went back on the road. "But grandmother gets paranoid when I try to bring up the topic," Ellie whined. "Don't care, she's the one you should be talking too, okay Ellie," he ended.

"Yes-Sir grandpa," as Ellie slouched down in the truck seat.

As they pull up to the Meyers, Ellie's heart starts racing again, as she floated out of the car. Mr. Meyers was already sitting out on the porch. "Samford and Ellie come and have a glass of lemonade made fresh today by Mrs. Meyers," said Mr. Meyers. "Will do made my throat is kinda dry from driving on that dusty road," said Mr. Samford. "Ma" yelled Mr. Meyers through the screen door. "Bring two big jars of lemonade for Mr. Samford and Ellie." "Well now Mr. Samford, while we wait on the drinks, tell me now; What you seen, What you heard and What you know?" As grandpa was just babbling out came Mrs. Meyers with the beverages and sat them down on the table she look at Ellie and said, "Ellie, be a dear and take this glass of lemonade to my son Israel around the back."

"Yes—Mam," said Ellie and was more than glad to fulfill Mrs. Meyers request except for one thing when she stood up to take the glass her legs begin wobbling and didn't want too cooperate. But she got them working again and she said to herself, "thank God, that the grownups hadn't even notice any difficulties with her legs." They just kept right on talking as she walked slowly toward the back, it seemed forever. Every step she took felt like she had on brick shoes.

Slowly she approached her gateway to heaven. She peaked at the beautiful structure temple. There he was, the city of Israel himself. His eyes glazing over his wax job on his brand new Desoto. She opened her mouth and fearfully nothing came out, unsuspectedly, she took a sip of his lemonade and finally at her destination she muttered a stale "hi."

He turned around took the glass of lemonade and took a big gulp then looked at her and gave her a big smile. "Miss Mahogany," that is what he always called Ellie. "Thank you, I don't know what made that lemonade so good. My mother making it or you bringing it to me in this yellow dress under this beautiful yellow sun we have. You know yellow is my favorite color?" Israel said. "It is?" said Ellie pretending to be surprised.

"Yap," Israel, took another sip from his glass of lemonade. "Hold that for me again," said Israel, but Ellie didn't hear him talking for she was in a daze. "Miss Maghony—Ellie—Ellie Ruth Samford!" Israel's voice increased.

"Huh?" finally said Ellie.

"Girl, where is your mind?" with a devilish smile, asked Israel. Ellie's thought started back wandering again. "Oh fornication—here I come", Ellie said to herself. Even though she had not totally found out what it all meant, but she did know that it had something to do with the birds and the bees. For her grandma always talks against it and the only time really when grandmother gave her granddaughter full attention was when she was making Ellie's favorite candy.

Southern Pralines

1.c granulated sugar	1/4tsp.salt
1.c brown sugar, packed	2 tbsp. butter
½c. light cream	1c pecan halves

Lightly butter a sheet of wax paper. Combine sugars, cream and salt in large saucepan. Cook over medium heat, stirring constantly, until mixture spins a thread about 2 inches long when dropped from a spoon. Stirring constantly until small amount of mixture dropped into very cold water forms a small ball, which flattens when removed from water. Remove from heat; cool 5 minutes. Beat mixture with wooden spoon until slightly thickened and candy just coats nuts, but does not lose its gloss. Drop candy by large spoonfuls onto buttered sheet of wax paper. Makes about 1 ½ dozen of candies.

Surely, Ellie grandmother's reasons had nothing to do with the man she called, "The Great Israel." At least she hoped not. For you couldn't ask for a better man to tutor any female around these parts about fornicating on this side of heaven in their little town called Eight Mile, Alabama. "Ellie?" again Israel asks. *{All in one breathe}* Ellie asked, "When, I turn thirteen this fall, do you think you can teach me about pleasures?" Israel stopped buffing his car and gave Ellie a blank look. He walked over and his face blocked the sun as he looked down at her. "What kind of pleasures?" he asked flashing his winning smile with those perfect white teeth of his.

{That Is When Ellie Ruth Samford Passed Out!}

"Mr. Samford, Dad, its Ellie come quick!" yelled Israel.

"My Lord," also running to the scene was Mrs. Meyers. "What happen to the chile?" asked Mrs. Meyers. "Heat!" answered Israel.

"Yap this sun will do it," said Mr. Meyers.

"Come on, Ellie it's time to take you home," said her grandfather while picking her up from her waist side. Slowly getting up, Ellie looked up and around and was so embarrassed, but Israel gave her an okay smile.

Some Are Structured Like
The Leaning Tower of Pisa

"Okay class—hush, settle down please, this chapter is about body odor and your body odor do not have to do with your age or your size. Which we have in here, it's all about glands, some people just have overactive glands that make them sweat and smell," said Mrs. Fowler, the classroom teacher.

"This chapter was written for you, Ervin," shouted Lloyd.

"Your mama," Ervin shouted back.

Bursts of laughters and Oo - -hs came from some of the classmates. Hastily, Lloyd stood up and said, "Boy—what you say about my mama?"

Also, Ervin stood up and said, "My humble apology, I forgot about your nappy headed & skank of a sister of yours also."

More laughter came from the classmates. Lloyd, jumped two desks over; not caring about the students he had trampled on, just to get to Ervin. "BI _ CH!" said Lloyd.

"Hey—Hey—Stop it," said Mrs. Fowler who had ran in between them. But Ervin already had his fists drawn up in the air. Mrs. Fowler, looked up and said "You better not mistakenly hit me boy or you'll meet Jesus today!" the third time the class burst out again with laughter, it was agreeable with the expressions on their faces that they had been surely entertained this morning. Mr. Briggs, the school principal, came in the classroom, because he heard the commotion outside as he was passing by. "Who started it this time Mrs. Fowler?" asked Mr. Briggs.

"As always, Ervin." Said Mrs. Fowler with frustration on her face.

"Come along, Ervin and by the time you get to this door, your attitude better had changed Black Boy!" Said Mr. Briggs'. Ervin knew he couldn't respond to his remark for he was already in deep trouble. But those that were out of ignorance knew the reason behind, Mr. Briggs's comment. Prejudice! Mr. Briggs' lighter pigmentation made him feel powerful over darkies.

"Okay the circus show is over," said Mrs. Fowler. "Please open your books again to the chapter of Body Odor. Phyllis begin reading."

"Yes—Mam" responded, Phyllis. While Phyllis was reading, Sam passed a note over to Ellie from Doris, it read. *{Are you going to walk home with us: Phyllis, Carmellette and I today? Nod your head for yes or no}* Ellie, look over to Doris and shook her head as a yes. Ellie didn't know why she agreed with that for the way they went it made her route home longer. But it was a beautiful day, God had used the big trees as a fan to blow across their little town as the slight wind danced off their faces and for that reason, the long stroll should be just fine. The bell finally rang and as all children who detest to be detained in one sitting they rushed out with cheer to see what kind of mischief they could get into.

Phyllis, Carmellette and Doris were already outside waiting for Ellie. Sam also was waiting with the group and as usual *{to be a boy}* always talking.

"Well, I heard that Mr. Briggs added all kinds of stuff on Ervin and even repeated some old stuff. I tell you when Ervin's uncle showed up at the school. He was like a mad dog that had rabies! They said in the middle of Mr. Briggs conversation, that Ervin uncle started beating him and then Mr. Briggs came from behind the desk and held Ervin down," ended, Sam.

"Whach you say?" said Carmellette.

"Mmh—Sho' did," ended, Sam.

"Why Those Sons Of Bit_ _es!" Carmellette responding to what her ears had just hear. Continuing she said, "And it's not all his fault. He's just venting out. Ervin is so far behind in his spelling and numbers it's a shame. No support from home and they work him in the fields like he is a slave." Sam said as he gave Carmellette a puzzled look.

"I'm missing something here, when did you become a Psychologist?"

"Since she started liking, Ervin." giggled Phyllis.

Carmellette defended her reason. "So what if I do?"

"That do better become a don't." With a cute order from Sam thought Phyllis to herself. "What?" asked Carmellette.

"You heard me—he'll be riding on your skirt tail, no future in that at all, he's not of your kind, better off without him, I'm telling you, leave him be," ended, Sam with his hand on his hip. Carmellette, look and tried to figure out what battle to pick first. Sam's hand on his hip or his stupid remark he just made. "He just needs some guidance and support," Carmellette decided to say.

"He just need to be left alone, ole stubborn—GAL!" Sam's voice increased.

"Who in the hell, you're calling GAL?" Carmellete, voice increased higher than Sam's. "You, Carmellette and this notion of yours; always wanting to help the needy, well you can't help everybody and women never going to be Principals."

Phyllis's face showed shock and she said. "a principal?"

Sam interrupted, "Crazy and stupid—huh?" "This town or any other town, especially in the state of Alabama, never going

21

to have a *{Feline}* principal. Let us take this moment and dissect that word *{pal}*. Pal means fellow and fellow means male. You will never hear females introducing each other as pals. Everybody knows that men make better administrators. The bible says: Let us make man and I don't recall, there are no female powerful rulers in the holy bible!" Carmellette readjusted her stand and said. "Now let me take a couple more moments and tell you that not only your brain is immature, but the muscle between your thigh is as well!" Phyllis, Doris and Ellie stood with their mouths open.

"Do you even have desires to find out?" asked Sam.

"Drop this—it's getting late," said Phyllis.

"Yeah, let's go," said Doris. Phyllis whispered a question to

Sam. "Are you okay?" Sam smiled at Phyllis and said, "I'm the future, I am a MAN—now go on."

As the group walked off, Sam hollered out to Carmellette. "Next you'll be saying that women will have their own Business, become Generals, Mayors and the President. Never, I say never!"

"Why do you debate with him and get him so upset?" asked, Phyllis.

"Practice—it was all practice!" answered Carmellette.

The group was quiet walking home; they all had their individual thoughts.

Ellie: Was thinking about Israel as usual.

Doris: Thinking of nothing in particular. Her childhood was partial. Meaning that at the age of nine, skipping rope and playing jacks had been way over for her.

With a mother, who had a nervous breakdown and an older sister who was too busy into herself. There was no father at her house, but in the church house. Yes there is a skeleton rumor that Pastor Caldwell is Doris's father and that her mother once upon a time was very active in all the church auxiliary clubs and being the head chairperson to practically all of them is the reason why she spent a lot of time in the pastor's study. So she was very needed. But the pastor had more needs than Phyllis's mother could apply. As a matter of fact three other additional women was helping Pastor Caldwell's needs. Which became a problem to Doris's mother also. She didn't mind being the other woman, but she was not going to tolerate him cheating on her any longer. "A married man should only have one mistress!" Now, some people may think that all of this didn't make any sense and it did not. That's why her mother had the nervous breakdown. So, Doris belief is that no man was worth all of that and no man is going to have a chance to break her heart. They can have fun under her skirt, but not take her heart. Her heart thought Doris, "was way too precious!"

That's why she cared not to visit her father even though he shares a house with God, big deal. He has not once visited her or the wind has not thus carried words of him asking about her and her well-being. So fair is fair.

Doris's favorite outlet is school, because nothing ever exciting happened at home. Her mother again in her ragged dress, hair un-combed, teeth not brushed, walking around the house saying, Psalm 89. Verse 15. *"I am afflicted and ready to die from my youth up: while I suffer thy terrors I am distracted."*

The only conclusion that Doris could come up with of why her mother was distracted in procrastinating of killing herself is that her mother was hoping that Pastor Caldwell would come back in her life. But had her mother look at herself lately? What if Pastor Caldwell just popped over and said, "hello". Maybe that surprise visit may give her mother a heart attack. "Well, that is a thought for getting her mother out of her damned misery," Doris thought. Maybe she should go and visit her daddy at his Father's house.

Carmellette: Was thinking about college, her counselor had already applied Carmellette and was approved to attend a summer class at Tuskegee University.   But Carmellette perception did not like what Mr. Booker T. Washington stood for.   She wanted a better education somewhere that would challenge her mind not challenge her hands! She also didn't appreciate her counselor sending a letter on her behalf and she let him know that she did not find that amusing.   Carmellette knew that if she keeps plucking at it that she would come across another university in reading or overhearing someone speak of it.

For, she was not getting anywhere with her counselor.   Her dreams were pursuing anything that dealt with politics. Carmellette wanted to change the *{Good O'l Boy}* system.   She was tired of men having their way.   God knows it is that way at her home.   Carmellette had no mother or any aunts to model after of how to act as a female.   Her family consisted of her older brother and their father.   Her mother died long time ago and her mother didn't have any sisters.   Naturally her father is the ruler in their home and when he wasn't there then her older brother thought that he was the ruler; making her not only do all the cooking, cleaning the house but killing the chickens.   Now her brother did not mind plucking the already dead chickens, too. But he did not have a stomach of killing them.   Maybe because he was a chicken himself! So, Carmellette had grown guts and maybe that's why she did not show feminine ways like certain women in the town thought she should have.   And this really bothered, Carmellette, but her mind was more than just to please

25

the town women. For in her opinion, they were stuck in the cave man days. About how a woman supposed to just lay there and get pulled by the hair and do his will. Well, Carmellette was not having it. She already knew. To beat a man in his own game one must think like a man. Practicing law was her future plan and determination is her ticket out.

Phyllis: Not surprised was thinking about Sam & his temper. She loved to watch him take charge and step forward as a man is supposed to. Crossing her fingers to be his wife and the mother of his children would suit her just find. She was taught that any men who accept challenges make great providers. Whether, they battered their women or not. *{Besides}* a man has to let off their steam some kind of way, from the dealings and financial decisions they make everyday for their family. Surely anyone could understand that. She did, now all she had to do is to convince Sam that his success is her success. Facial attraction was not what Phyllis had. Along with that, she didn't have good posture, nor a pretty voice and she has big feet. If she pinned up her hair in a ball and wore an over sized loose blouse to hide the little breast she had, hell she would look like a man. Her only chance of getting a man was to show him that she was a Christian. A Christian woman most likely will do right by her man and not display herself as a whore. Yet she was a whore. Last summer she left to take care of her all of a sudden stricken ill aunt who lived in another state. Yet it was the other way around, her aunt became the new mother of Phyllis's little baby girl.

You would think that, Phyllis had nightmares or some type of saddens about what she had done. But she didn't. Her heart was just that cold. You're talking about turning the other cheek. It seemed like, Phyllis done got confused about the bible or is it that Phyllis and a whole lot of other Christians out there used the bible solely to justify their twisted up lives. To make them feel better and a part of being one step ahead of an atheist.

Finally, Carmellette broke the silence, because the group was at her house. "See you pals—later." Said Carmellete, the rest of the group just looked at her. "Oh never mind forget it!" Carmellette stormed off. Not really caring Doris, Phyllis and Ellie resumed their journey again with silence. They were about to pass the Osborne's property. The Osborne's kept a lot of broken and old junk in their yard. The group saw the youngest son, Kerrie Osborne, who was sitting on a broken down wagon, finishing up on a bottle of moonshine which was strong enough to kill a mound of ants and the queen ant herself. Yet, it was known that Kerrie could hold his liquor and run 3 miles with the scorching sun beaming on him and not even pass out! "Ellie, this is not your route—going home," said Kerrie.

"My route is what I choose to be," Ellie, sassed back.

Kerrie just smiled, "Oh excuse my manners, ladies have some?" Holding out the bottle towards them.

"You mean drink from the same bottle?" asked Doris.

Phyllis' elbow gave Doris a bump on her arm and Doris bumped her back with her elbow. Kerrie, pretended not to notice, but kept on talking. He jumped down from the broken wagon and said, "You're right, forgive me, I'm just showing lousy manners today."

"Come on lets go get a cup." Kerrie was walking back to the house and before Doris could plant one step in the ground to follow Kerrie Phyllis pulled Doris by her ponytail scarf and said, "Get Back Here!"

"You better let go of me—I feel safe, I'm just going to get a cup!" Doris, pulling away from, Phyllis' grip.

"And what else?" Hollered out, Phyllis.

But, Doris did not turn around to respond, but kept right on going. "Maybe we should go with, Doris?" asked Ellie.

"No we shouldn't and she shouldn't either," said Phyllis.

"Well you couldn't stop her, for some reason she's very adamant about that cup," Ellie said to Phyllis.

"I don't know why she's going. She has never tried that stuff before. Have you?" asked Phyllis.

"Nope," answered Ellie. "Then why did she go?" said Phyllis out loud to the sky.

"So she can try it," said Ellie, also out loud to the sky. Wandering what the heck Phyllis was looking at to make her look up. "Well, I'm not gonna stand around here, while she go get a cup of whiskey *{Like that really offended her}*. Let's go Ellie," said Phyllis walking away. Phyllis, not feeling Ellie's presence behind her, turn around. Ellie was still standing at the same spot. "Ellie, I said lets go."

"Somebody, gotta be here—I'm going to try to wait. Go on, responded Ellie.

"What ever!" said Phyllis with her hands in the air in disgust.

"Kerrie—where are you?" asked Doris as she walked in the house, she would have knocked but there was no door and no evidence that there was going to be a door any time soon. Kerrie's voice came from the rear of the house. "In the kitchen—just come straight to the back." Doris followed Kerrie's instructions. There she found Kerrie standing by the sink. "Grab that chair, bring it over here, then stand on it and

29

reach inside that top cabinet. We're going to use my mama's china cups. This calls for a special celebration," said Kerrie.

"Ooh a special celebration," Doris said to herself. She didn't know why, but it sounded good to her and she grabbed the chair that Kerrie pointed to. Then Doris drag the chair to the kitchen sink, stood on it and *{simultaneously and slowly}* as she glided her arms up, Kerrie glided his hand up on her leg, then Doris reach to the top of the shelf, while Kerrie reach inside of Doris's undergarment, then Doris fingers poke inside the cabinet and loop and reached further in the cabinet for a china cup. Then Kerrie poke his finger inside of Doris unexplored vagina, Doris wiggle a little and Kerrie finger wiggle deeper in as his breath was panting saying "Don't move." She stood there on the chair, then again she didn't know what else to do. She wasn't scared or anything like that. But what Kerrie was doing to her was all-new and slightly uncomfortable. All of this for a cup of whiskey she thought. Doris then felt wetness below; she didn't know whether or not she had pead or what? At any rate whatever it was, Kerrie seem not to mind. Now she felt two of his fingers move in a rapid speed, in and out, as his fingers and now his face under her skirt greedily continue to fondle her vagina as his tongue licked and tickled her clitoris.

Not fearing of falling, yet she held on to the cabinet handle *{tight}* as her heart rate increased and then unexplannedly she taste her blood from the bottom of her lip from where she bit. More than a few seconds passed without, Doris thinking of anything. Where did her mind go? Doris couldn't think of anything, for the first time her mind went blank. But still confused, Kerrie then let out a loud moan.

Then *{simultaneously and slowly}* the two reached for each other and hug, while Kerrie, beg for forgiveness'. And Doris did.

Experience is Essence…Regardless

"Put away your book, to take your English quiz," said Mrs. Fowler.

"Ah—ah," said some of the students in Ellie's classroom. Mrs. Fowler took her ruler and slaps it on her desk. "Anymore comments like that from anybody, I hear or even see automatically will receive minus five points from their quiz. Now there are three questions on the chalkboard, answer each question in a complete paragraph. Spelling, Structure and use proper Sentences. All of that will count toward your grade. Now you have fifth-teen minutes, that is five minutes to each question. Please start."

In the middle of the quiz, Sam passed a note from Doris to Ellie and before Ellie could read it Mrs. Fowler who saw the whole note passing exchange said, "Ellie, bring me that note. You and Doris can just walk up to the principal's office right now!" The rest of the students looked in silence as Doris and Ellie got up from their desks and walked out.

"Ricky," continued Mrs. Fowler as she was writing something on the back of the note, "take this cheating note to Mr. Briggs the school principal and you better not look at it.

Any work from Doris, that in tells is a low grading in it self. Now hurry back," sighing Mrs. Fowler.

"Yes-Mam." Said Ricky as he walked out of the classroom. The whole class was now starring at Mrs. Fowler. "Stop looking at me, I know I'm beautiful—finish taking your quiz." Instantly, the whole class buried their head in their quiz.

Ellie and Doris were sitting outside of the principal's door when Ricky came up. "Mrs. Fowler, wrote a note too on the back of your note," said Ricky. Doris tried to snatch the note from Ricky's hand.

"What does it say?" asked Doris. But Ricky was faster than Doris hand.

"You forgot to say please," said Ricky continuing. "And by the way you don't snatch anything out of anybody's hand, especially when you're in trouble," Ricky ended.

"Stop messing around—what do the note say?" impatiently asked Doris.

"Ricky, stop clowning around and head back to class young man."

Ricky didn't have to turn around to know whose voice that was. "Yes—Sir," said Ricky and he walked back to class as he was told.

"You gals follow me in my office," said Mr. Briggs. As he sat leaned in his recliner, Ellie and Doris sat in the available chairs. Ellie was still in the dark of what was going on. For she didn't know what the note really had said for she never got a chance to read it. Mr. Briggs sat up in his recliner and said. "I'm puzzled," Continuing he said. "Doris explain."

Doris shrugged her shoulders and replied. "Don't know - Sir."

Mr. Briggs face became red, cause his pigmentation can do that. "Doris do you think, I have time to waste?" asked the principal.

"Don't know—Sir." Doris replied again. Mr. Briggs stood from behind his desk angrily and said, "Doris, bend over and touch your toes, Ellie wait out side." You didn't have to tell Ellie twice, but Ellie was very concerned for Doris' sake. She didn't like the sound of Mr. Briggs voice. Come to think of it deep inside, she really did not care for his character at all. Maybe it was all the rumors she had heard about him. But she had to do what she was told. For they were taught as children, you do what grownups say and no questions asked!

"I said SQUAT—Doris," said Mr. Briggs. Doris squatted. Mr. Briggs taking his paddle from the wall then came behind his desk. "No not that way, I'll teach you - you black wench.

Touch your toes, arch those legs up, stick your butt up in the air, and {yes} just like that." He raised her skirt, pulled down her undergarment and as he pulled it down his thumb rolled down in the center crease of her butt. It was black, smooth, and beautiful. He stood by the side of her face. Doris noticed a bulge in his pants and was not sure how it got there. But she was quickly brought back to her unfortunate dilemma that she had some how put herself in. "Say it, Doris, say, I'm naughty," said Mr. Briggs. Poor confused Doris said "I'm naughty" and that is when Mr. Briggs gave her a swap on her butt, so hard that it almost tilted Doris over and the tears just swelled in Doris eyes. "Say it again—you black wench," as Mr. Briggs bulge from his pants pressed harder on the side of Doris's face.

"I'm naughty." Doris repeated.

Whap! Another, swap on her butt from Mr. Briggs's paddle, now the tears rolling down on Doris face.

"Ah—what's the matter, Doris, those little pops hurt your butt?" asked Mr. Briggs. Doris throat was so choked up that she couldn't speak, so she nodded her head up and down as a yes motion. "Well—now let me rub the sting off." Mr. Briggs put his paddle down to rub her butt, squeezing each butt cheek and rub lower playing with her vaginal hair. How surprised he was to feel that it was soft as her butt cheek. He was already excited.

{His wife never could turn him on like this} Rubbing his hand and fingers down and up on her butt. And *{yes}* finally her body responding to his touches as he felt her sticky juices on his fingers. Oh it must be so nice to be a youth, just look at her still in the same arch position, not given way at all. *{He said to himself}* her sticky juice on his thumb enter her tight anus.

Even though her nipples got on hard and itch with joy, Doris said. "No - please."

But, Mr. Briggs didn't hear her. Fuc_ing her anus with his thumb, oh God how he wanted so badly to do more. Did this young girl know what she did to men, did she know she made men buckled to their knees, did she know if he could he would take his stiff rod caressing and stroke from her vagina to her anus. Stroking, caressing, back, forth, in and out. Hot damn, he was in another world.

With his other hand, Mr. Briggs tilted Doris face and he lick and kiss her ears, as it was her lips and searching for the back of her throat. After a few more seconds pass by again, Doris heard the same familiar moan, but this time it came from Mr. Briggs. He barely stood up; the excitement was just a little bit too much for him. His paces were like a turtle as he walked back to his recliner and sat down in it, he then leaned back in the recliner and stared out side his office window. "Get situated—gal and I don't want to see you back in my office again!"

Doris, pulled up her undergarment and her skirt down. "Yes—Sir," she said to the principal and left his office. Surprised, she found Ellie, still waiting for her. "You mean you stuck around this time." Said Doris.

"Doris, I'm sorry what did your note say?" asked Ellie.

Doris replied. "About yesterday—but never mind, I got something else to add on to that note. But no more passing notes from this day forward, I tell you all about it at lunch. And the two went back to class.

__Automatic Tribulation!__

{I WANT YOU} The poster read with Uncle Sam's picture on it. Holding up the picture. "This is how they eliminate our brothers!" Holding the poster up higher and then ripping it in half. "World War II, our brothers came back as broke privates," Said, Kerrie at the podium. The Church was used often as the town meeting place. The rest of the men sat in the church and listened and agreed by shaking their heads. Kerrie continue. "And Mel Junior, still hasn't gotten his recognition and may never get it. Go on Mel and tell us what happen," said Kerrie. "Well," Mel Junior standing up and start speaking, "stupid as it may sound, but true story, it was our own man, who threw a practice grenade the wrong way. A white boy, with a good left arm, good enough to be in pro baseball. Well anyhow he threw the grenade toward the ammunition storage and it ricochet by some gasoline barrels. Needless do, I need to say anymore. But damn fireworks everywhere! Back in those days we could only just supervise in cooking, cleaning and watching the graveyard shift without protection. I was the assistant cook and through the mess hall kitchen window, I saw compounds of smoke and fire headed my way. I told them white boys that if they didn't want to be bake like kapuns, these here young roosters I got in the oven, then ya'll better follow me.

Later on, the Lieutenant came in our barrack and walked to my bunk."

"Attention," he said.

I stood in formation, like a soldier supposed to and the Lieutenant said to me with a grin. "Cadet, what is it this I'm hearing, tell me it couldn't be true?" asked the Lieutenant. With proud in my face, I answered "Yes—Sir."

The Lieutenant walked a complete circle around and stood behind me. Put his hand on my right shoulder, with his left hand, leaned forward over, as he leaned his right leg went slightly up and he spit tobacco on my right boot! Straighten back up to a perfect balance and he said, "Now that is what I call a perfect formation." Then about two feet or so of him walking away the Lieutenant turned around and said, "Oh kitchen boy, thank you for saving my men."

Mel Junior, rubbing his hands together, "it took me the all of God's powers not to hit that asshole, stripes or no stripes!" As Mel Junior, sat back down. Kerrie stood back at the podium again and said, "see what I'm saying, in their war we will never get respect. It's stupid, it's Fuc_ ed and it's"

Pastor Caldwell interrupted, sitting with the rest of the men and pointed to Kerrie.

"Wo—Wo, son you're in a church house. Now, I did not call this meeting for us to become rebels. This meeting was called to decide, how are we going to alert and inform our own women on the sudden changes we're having. Who are scared especially the ones that won't have a man or another mature male around, when the head household go off to war. We have to go to WAR! It is part of our responsibility as Americans and for sure nothing won't change if we do not participate."

Rudely, Kerrie interrupted. "We didn't ask to come over here—we were taken from our homes from the mother land who used to love us and we loved her!" Then Sam stood up and said, "I am so sick of hearing tired brothers like you, talking about the mother land and knowing damn well, if they drop your ass off their tonight, you wouldn't know what to do, but cry out for your mama, like a baby suckin' on a titty!" The men in the church burst out laughing. Kerrie, calmly looked at Sam and said, "Funny a big roar, coming from a cub bear." The men in the church burst out laughing again. Sam looked at Kerrie and before he could offered a rebuttal, Israel who was also sitting down with the rest of the men spoke up and said. "Sam, sometimes silence is golden."

Sam sat back down again.

Deacon Lincoln then stood up and he was tall, skinny and face drawn in, just like president Lincoln except, Deacon Lincoln is colored. Around here they say, some of the free slaves took the name Lincoln as gratitude, because he freed the slaves.

Anyway, Deacon Lincoln cleared his throat and said. "We are in a War, whether we like it or not, it affects us, whether we like it or not. There is no big rock to hide under or anything for us to hide behind. Our colored women are not weaklings like you want them to be. If a white woman can leave and work in a off base military camp to provide some kind of revenue for her family, because she will then be the head household than surely our colored women can and will too. Times are hard, but not as hard as the Twenties. We that lived in the country, hell the twenties behind the stock market crashing did not affect us any shape, form or fashion. Because we were already poor! We were already struggling and we're still struggling and unfortunate because as long as we are this color, *{Deacon Lincoln, pulling back his shirtsleeve from one of his arm}* we will always struggle. Yet by and by we will have finer things in life, but we will still struggle to keep a place of peace, to keep an identity, to keep lifting our voice to be heard and to keep fighting for our children's respect and education. Struggling and Patience is what we know how to do best if nothing at all. Our *{white*

41

cousins} are going to make damn sure of that. Nevertheless, God is on our side and for that reason alone this is how we go forward, find and fetch our future in this land that we call America."

You Talking About Grown Men Crying!

Thank you, Lincoln…Thank you.

The Puss' And The Rabbit

"I'm going to the Navy," said Ervin. "Why?" asked Carmellette.

"Yeah, I'm leaving tonight, I'm going to be a steward," Ervin continued.

Carmellete, wraped her arms around, Ervin. "Please don't go."

Ervin, put a distance between him and Carmellette. "Girl, I didn't know you was going to act like this."

"Kiss me," asked Carmellete. But before, Ervin got a chance to respond, Carmellette reached over anyway and {*aggressively*} start kissing him on his lips, neck and ears. "Carmellete, what are you doing?" Ervin pushed Carmellete away from him.

"I'm trying," said Carmellete.

"What?" asked Ervin.

"I'm trying to do this, let me do this, I need to do this," begged Carmellete.

"Do what?" asked Ervin.

Carmellete, reached and took off Ervin's shirt, his biceps chest and stomach now out in view. Then she dropped her dress,

43

showing of her already mature body and lay on a bed of hay; spread her legs like a new butterfly ready to take off. "You got no britches on!" stuttered, Ervin. Carmellete, motion her finger to lie on top of her. Ervin felt a sensation of heat, which almost made him pass out. "Ervin what are you waiting on?" Carmellette asked.

"My feet," said Ervin. "Well tell your feet to come on." Said Carmellete.

"Okay feet—come on," said, Ervin, and he took off running home!

<u>*"Baby Brown"*</u>

If it wasn't for my "Baby Brown" eyes

a corner of my thoughts wish he never exist

If I knew his strut continued to have nightmares to them

my "Baby Brown" eyes would had never exist

If I knew behind his smile had more lies than his set of teeth

my "Baby Brown" eyes would had never exist

If I only just took heed of what I painfully come to realize now

my "Baby Brown" eyes would had never exist

He too

(the father of my child)

has "Brown" eyes

but they look out with

Disappointments, Disrespect and Aggravation!

Self-love he only has

And with that in mind, knowing that he's roaming around—

Alive

my stomach will continue twist and foul up

"Baby Brown"

"Baby Brown"

So gentle, so smart and ever so beautiful

regardless

I will always love thee my "Baby Brown"

45

Retired Gypsy

a retired gypsy is gladly what i am.

no more ugly wives hating me, knowing that their husbands idolize at me to satisfy their desires...no more insecure girlfriends have the audacity to approach me with disbeliefs, because their boyfriends adore me the most...no more receiving false compliments from men just to bed with me...no more women rolling their eyes at me or try to be friends with me so that they can learn my secrets of doing what i did best.

See Gypsies Turn All Heads!

a gypsy pays a heavy price to be pretty, being the entertainer and to be love only by her body...the seekers care less about her mind that is why a gypsy get the end of the short stick...yet a new dawn begins and a gypsy rise with rejoicing fire.

For She Is Love By Two Gods!

jehovah and lucifer...that is why she can not help her life being rocky and with constant drama, because those two men have her in their little tug a war game

back n forth she is pulled her soul hurts more so than her body from their pulling.

a retired gypsy is not because she gave birth for she's still a silly creative child within...and certainly not because of marriage for a true gypsy is really married to herself.

A True Gypsy!

like me is glad that retirement has finally sat in...now all i do is sit back and enjoy of being in the shadows and console the young gypsies.

Both Em' Eyes Open Now

I couldn't believe what I just read. A *"Retired Gypsy and Baby Brown"* poem written by *"Ivory Estrada"* grandma is a poet and mix? I always thought she and her sisters just had good hair! Nicaragua is a word that I heard one time around here, I had broken this little vase. Of course it was an accident. But grandma, didn't care she whooped me so with the switch she made from the willow tree. It left scars on me.

She was mad, because I had broken the vase from Nicaragua. I have broken a piece of her memory from her native home. Oh, so ever precious Nicaragua! Now I know why our brown rice that we eat is a little different then anybody else's around here and why grandma sometimes at night read this little black book. I thought for a long time that it was the Holy Bible. Until one day, I opened it up and stuttered on the first word, I couldn't pronounce it. I took it to my grandma and asked her, to help me to pronounce the words that were in the book. She kindly took the book away from me and said, "this book is for me and only for me, it helps me not to forget," and concealed the little black book in her apron pocket.

Instead this time with my questions, I'm going to ask Aunt Effie.

I'm sure; I will get better luck this time. Ellie ran upstairs and as usual Aunt Effie was always in her room. Where else will she be? She didn't cook, clean or even help with washing. Besides, her sister Ivory, always saying she got it. Aunt Effie's door was always slightly open. Ellie pushed the door wider. There she saw her Aunt Effie, reading. Aunt Effie love to read, she will read anything that she got her hands on or any print her eyes saw. Even if the words were on a building, sidewalk, and furniture. A walking book is what she is.

"Aunt Effie, may I show you something?" asked Ellie.

"Sure Caterpillar," Said her Aunt Effie.

That is what her Aunt Effie from day one called Ellie when she moved in with The Samford's home. She said that Ellie was a moth in hibernation and just waiting for the cycle to complete so that she can show the world how beautiful a butterfly Ellie had become. Then, Ellie will take off and fly closer to her destiny!

"Continue", said Aunt Effie. "Yes—Mam, what reason can I help you today?" Ellie smiled, looked and asked, "how do you know it's a reason?" Aunt Effie got up and took her niece Ellie by the hand and they both looked in the mirror. "Why you don't see it?" asked her Aunt Effie. "See what?" asked Ellie.

"See the big {*C's*} on your face?" laughed Aunt Effie. "{*C's*}?" said Ellie.

"Yes {*C's*} for Curiosity the Caterpillar." And started tickling Ellie.

They laugh for a moment, until Ellie showed the papers to her aunt.

"Aunt Effie, read this." Ellie handed the papers to her aunt.

Her aunt quickly looked over the papers and her smile became a frown. "I don't have to read all of it, where did you get this?" asked her aunt.

"Well, I wasn't snooping or anything like that," said Ellie. "You heard my question, where did you get this?" her Aunt's voice now with firmness.

"In a bag," said Ellie.

"What bag?" asked her Aunt Effie.

"In the stairway closet, I was looking for some yarn," said Ellie and she thought about maybe her luck would have been better if she asked about the poems to her grandmother instead of Aunt Effie, because her aunt drilling questions made her scared.

"Yarn for what?" Aunt Effie kept on asking.

"For a project, a collage that I have to do for class, did I do anything wrong?" asked Ellie.

"If you think you wasn't doing anything wrong then why are you showing me these poems instead of your grandmother?"

More questions from her aunt. "I don't know," said Ellie.

And before Ellie knew it, her aunt gave her a pop in the face with the two poems that Aunt Effie had somehow previously rolled together with out Ellie noticing.

"Stop that damn crying you liar!" commanded her aunt.

"But, I'm not lying." Ellie ducked with her arms over her face. For her aunt was about to give her another pop until Ellie said "okay, I'm lying." Ellie would have said anything not to get another pop. Aunt Effie sat Ellie on her bed and pull up her reading chair. "Look at me, Ellie," Aunt Effie, continued. "This is our secret, this is a side that your grandmother does not want you to ever see. There is not a night she cries about your mother, her daughter. Your grandmother at one time or another was a very free spirit. Once upon a time, she loved dancing, drinking, drugging. Living a daring life not caring about tomorrow and did not give a damn about yesterday. She got pregnant, she dealt with it and Mr. Samford stopped being one of her night clients and started being her husband.

He brought her here and ever since then, she's been here, she enjoys being here and she will die here!"

"So grandpa is not my -?" And before Ellie could finish her question, her aunt rose up again with her hand in a strike position.

"Not your what—surely you're not talking about the man that has grown old and now have a bad back busting his ass providing for your grandmother, your mother and you? I dare you to say it, you'll never make it to your thirteenth birthday!" Her aunt putting her arm down and in a calm voice said. "Ellie, my Caterpillar, the wonderful thing about mistakes is that our life would not be complete without them. *{Surviving your mistakes makes ones identity}* if you only remember one thing that I tell you. Please remember that one and that quote will take you further than any mountains you can see. And as you grow older and wiser into womanhood—trust me. Love will come through many different people even if they are not your blood relatives." Her Aunt Effie, kissed her forehead and said, "Now let's plan for your birthday party."

Possibility

"Happy Birthday to you, Happy Birthday to you, Happy Birthday to Ellie, Happy Birthday to you, and many more. Yeah – Congratulations," Everybody said, after they had sung the birthday song. "Okay, blow out the candles o'l lady," said Israel. Some of the party guests started laughing, behind Israel's joking comment. Even though you only supposed to have one birthday wish, Ellie partially cheated. She made a wish with an extension on it.

Her wish was that she can finally receive a kiss from the Great Israel and the extension was whereever Ervin was that hopefully he would be found. For the last person that saw him was Carmellette and she said that something scared him to run off.

But run where? Is the question this town has been asking? Not only that but Carmellette has put on some pounds since that day. Which got the town wandering, what did happen when those two last met. Ervin is gone for them to ask and Carmellette has sunk into a deep depression. And when you mention about boys around her, she start crying and caring on. Saying. "Why me, Lord, why me?" So with that in mind, Ellie was not going to share her wish about kissing Israel.

No surprise, Pastor Caldwell grabbed the cake knife and said, "Let me help you Ellie." But instead, he cut a big slice and served himself first. Then spoke out, "I'm still growing," with a big grin on his face and walked away from the table. Somehow, Israel got Ellie's attention. Ellie handed the cake knife duty to somebody else. Israel walked outside, Ellie a couple of steps behind him, and then she saw Israel sit in the swing that hung from the big oak tree.

"Push me," He said as Ellie walk nearer to him.

"Push you?" asked, Ellie.

"Yeah, you got some kind of strength, I saw you handle that cake knife, feeding those sugar teeth wolves in there Like a pro," Israel chuckled.

"I will push you, once I get my pretty please," Ellie sassed back.

"Now, why do I need to say something that you already know?" asked Israel.

"You want the push or not?" Ellie asked.

"Is that the same yellow dress you passed out in?" That question from Israel, made Ellie hot and she stormed off, but Israel grab her by the waist and she fell into Israel's lap. Now the two both sitting on the swing.

He pulled her hair back from her shoulder and softly kissed the back of her neck. Ellie was waiting to pass out, but she didn't. Instead she displayed all her teeth from her grin.

"Do you think you can teach me about pleasures?" asked Israel.

Ellie in a daze said. "Ah—huh."

Israel pushed her and him off the swing. She did not feel his grip on her side for she felt like feathers floating in the sky. He touched Ellie's lip with his finger and then kissed her. It was a long kiss that Ellie had to break away for air.

"What's wrong, you got eleven more kisses to be an official Thirthteen," Said Israel.

Ellie stepped back. "It seems like, I've been waiting all my life for this and that day is here, right now, in these moments and I don't feel right." Looking away.

"Because, you're nervous, it's going to be okay—trust me— I promise," said Israel.

"No it's not nervous, it's wrong—we're not married!" as Ellie looked away.

"You're right—I'm sorry, since we had eleven more kisses to go, how about the eleventh of next month?" and ending with those words, Israel got down with one knee.

Ellie still not looking and not hearing a word of what he just said, but did notice Phyllis, Doris, Carmellete and Sam looking out from the house window with their mouths in shock. It was, Doris that pointed her finger down that made Ellie look. Slowly, Ellie turned to Israel and thought she was dreaming seeing Israel in that position.

"Well, how about it, will you marry me?" asked Israel.

Ellie smiled and touched Israel's cheek with her finger and said.

"Not until you say pretty please." Ellie sassed back.

"Now why will I tell you something you already know. Mrs. Ellie Ruth Meyers," and her husband Israel finally completed their eleven kisses in front of happy witnesses at Greater "*White*" Missionary Baptist Church.

<u>Long Days Ahead</u>

"Okay—okay. Marrying, Israel would have been the phenomenal wish, but you had to admit it would have been nice. When I get a chance, I will talk to Carmellete about her mission of being equal to a man. Around here, there is a name that they call those kinds of women!

Also, secretly, I would like to see my mother and talk with her. I will not be complete, to understand me. Until, I understand her.

Take Your Knives Or Scissors And Follow Me

Come now and let us throw black rose petals on shadow—TRUTH from their heads and to their feet

Barbeque their lies and show all your available teeth on darken hours

Come now and let us cripple these living moments—FORSAKE yesterday and by pass tomorrows

Come now and spit venom on trust

And drilled hate moments in ourselves

Come now and love the bulimia battle—PAIN REJECTION

Flourish is the highlights of death for whatever it is worth?

Come now and concentrate on others corruption (childhood devils never do learn)

Failure is their inner strength and they pacifies the ugliness about their lost souls

Come now and see what blind people view on disguised demons. Angels with cut wings

Fakes of human beings and the dead spirit that joins them

Come now and let us sit with each other

Flap our lips with un-disbelief gossip and leave with more hatred from where whence we came

Come now and hold my hands and I will hold your hands

The two of us, the three of us, the four of us and as our group gets larger

The benefits of this pain we will not let ourselves sacrifice ourselves to feel anymore

EXPAND YOUR EARLOBES

You come to cut—to slash the past?

NO POINTS FOR COURAGE HERE

Because, unfortunately, you can not destroy this—ROCK that was thrown at you

Not with these household tools

So pick up the rock and display it with the rest of your "Whatnots"

For this hurt cannot heal, but it will make you go forward!

Practicing And Preaching Should Go Together

"Since Jesus experienced pain then we too have to experience pain. But, Jesus had a choice and he made his decision". Doris was hearing him and not hearing him. To her Pastor Caldwell was just moving his mouth. Pastor Caldwell continues, "How thoughtful, of him to come down and live like humans for a little while and his grand exit will be forever known!"

"Whoop tee do," said Doris to her father, Pastor Caldwell.

He looks at her long and hard. He had to admit to himself that she did have his eyes and smile. Yet she came with anger and he was not in the mood or about to have a confrontation with an angry teenager who really should be mad with her mother instead. All of this anger could be settled if Doris would just seek out God's help.

Who do not judge a man. Just deal with his sin and that sin could be forgiven; because the sin is not the man it is an act by a man. After he repents, his shaky soul is healed once more. Can I get an amen?

"Hell no!" said, Doris out loud.

"I beg your pardon" asked Pastor Caldwell.

"I heard what you were just thinking" said Doris.

"Oh, so now you are a mind reader?" asked Pastor Caldwell.

"Your mind is very easy to read, I don't have to be a psychic. If only my mother wasn't so damn stupid, behind men," said Doris.

"I do not allow profanity in my chamber," replied Pastor Caldwell.

"You're right, only seducing women. Making them feel good. You are a gigolo; you would marry all of them if you could. Only God knows why your wife stays around. Bless her heart with all of your cheat'en and outside children past and recent ones. Does she really have that much low self-esteem about her? What is she gaining from all of this? Just to say, she got a man. Do she feel proud, like she had conquered something, than what the other women could not do and that was to get you down the wedding aisle. Anybody can marry a fool, especially if that fool doesn't have morals. I don't know about the rest of the other women you left your seed in, but you need to apologize to my mother. Oh' how you manipulated her. Sad to say, she still loves you!" Doris then, breathes out.

"I can't do that," replied Pastor Caldwell.

"Why not?" asked Doris.

"Because, I still love her. It's even a sin to think about your mother, but I can't help it. She has uniqueness' about her more so than my wife. I can't visit her, I am afraid of what would happen," said Pastor Caldwell.

Even though, Doris really did not mean what she had said earlier about wishing her mother's death. If he had just suddenly pop over without an invitation, but she did want to know what he was thinking about would happen. So, she asked.

"What would happen?"

A big grin came on Pastor Caldwell's face.

"It would take seconds and we would be in each other's arms. And all bad feelings would dissolve the moment we would kiss," said Pastor Caldwell.

"You really are a fool." said Doris angrily.

"Love is being a fool," said Pastor Caldwell.

"Well, your wife is that way, but my mother is not and, I'm going to help her pull herself out of this rut she's in. She's too beautiful to let herself go behind a man who's been around town more than three times. You keep your fond memories about my mother to yourself and when God comes and gets you, to cast you in the lake of fire, I hope your bible will be on page. Number 15. Verse.31. *Because he hath despised the word of the*

Lord and hath broken his commandment, that soul shall utterly be cut off; his iniquity shall be upon him. Before I go, let me now apologize for not going to your funeral. You should understand my distant feelings," said Doris.

"We have to do what we have to do," replied Pastor Caldwell.

"Your wife is not lucky," said Doris.

"Can you count on your hands how many wives are lucky? But they don't complain to hard and to loud or they would be by themselves. Continuous embarrassment is worst than being alone! For loneliness can kill a person inside and eventually show on the outside. And if they feel threatened that loneliness could appear in their lives. Then sometimes absurd actions will come out of that in secure humans. Now if you would excuse me, I have a memo to get out to my Deacons about Ervin's surprised death. But before you go, you tell your mama for me, that before I do close my eyes, we will speak again and whatever happens - happens. You, my namesake wife or other people's opinions is not going to stop us. You cannot stop *{real}* love. You can stop caring for somebody, but love is very haggling and you don't have to understand that because you were not around when we met. You're just public proof of what we had; mentally still have and the rest is yet to come. I'm not being vain, just speaking the truth and if there weren't any circumstances, in the way then we would have probably been still together. But circumstances can be removed. Right now, I'm in a content mode," grinned Pastor Caldwell.

"You are remarkable, I'm starting to believe you," said Doris while walking out. On the way home, she thought, her poor mama. She for sho' must help her poor mama now if this man is thinking about snooping around again. She was sorry for even visiting him. She should have left well enough alone. Well her mama was not going to be his bed victim again. Not if she could help it. If anything, she's going to help her mama get even. Mama needs to go and get her soul sanctified again.

It's nothing like good o'l church mess! Doris, geet'en wet and hot, in her panties just think'en about it. I can see it now Mrs. Caldwell on the piano, Pastor Caldwell in the pulpit and mama just got struck with the Holy Ghost. Just testifying away. Everything she knows about whose sleeping with whom, that there is two finance record books, about that crooked bible he holds. Shaken' toward the congregation with his crooked hands and that he wears a vegetable squash in his pants so that he looks like he got someth'en down there. Mama said that a white man could put him to shame. Now that's kindda sad thought Doris, laughing to her self.

Sex And Fun Have Three Letters Each

Our porch is very beautiful. My grandpa Samford made it. Another addition that he added to enhance the house. The porch is not square or rectangle it's a half crescent shape. The measures are 13 x 7 feet and 43 ½ inches in height. Beautiful because of it's.

- Unique shape.
- There are two entrance steps on each side.
- A primordial oval stained glassed picture of The Virgin Mary holding Baby Jesus.

But now after all of these years for the first time, I exactly viewed the stained glass picture. The woman and the baby are multi cultural. Nicaraguan and Colored. Just like my grandmother and you can tell by the clothes and hair, it's not European. After all these years this household celebrates and worship under the Baptist doctrine. But now, I'm un-puzzled and un-confused about having a catholic stained glass biblical picture. Because it's not!

And that black book she carries in her apron it's not a small bible. It's phrases, songs and poems from her native home.

Since my grandmother had caught up with her housework she decided to braid—corn roll my hair. But this time no curl bang in the front. She says, now I am young lady and thirteen years old—they don't supposed to be wearing curl bang and bunch of ribbons in their hair. Now is the time, better than anytime, I told myself. So, I asked the question.

"Grandma, what is heat?"

My grandma just kept braiding my hair and then she started humming her song.

{Lord don't move that mountain} Before she got to the second stanza, I asked her again, but a little louder, because perhaps she didn't hear me. Maybe she was in her own deep thoughts or just maybe going deaf, but mostly because she was still humming.

"I'm not talking about, science heat, I'm talking about heat, between a man and a woman?" I said.

She stopped!

She stopped humming and she stopped braiding my hair.

Instead my grandmother pointed out her finger to a pack of dogs crossing our property as she was pointing she said, "Ellie, you see those dogs over there?"

I said, "Yes-em"

She continued, "Well, the front dog is a Bitch and the rest of the dogs are males after that one female bitch. When you see a male human dog running behind you, you do exactly what that female dog is doing. Keep walking! For surely if you stop then you will know what heat is all about."

Then she started humming that same song all over again.

Damn, that's why I hate asking her anything. My grandmother take simple questions and answered them in parables. Now, I'm more confused than ever.

I know, I'll ask Doris at bible study. *{To our surprise, lately she's been coming, I wonder what are her reasons and bet you she got reasons}*

Anyway, we meet at the Henderick's place. Where usually bible study is hosted along with Sister Henderick's pork chops. Where nobody is ashamed to lick their fingers and suck on the pork chop bones right afterwards.

"It was spitting!" said Doris.

"Spitting how?" asked Carmellette.

As Ellie walked in, Doris was spitting.

"Why is she spitting?" asked Ellie.

"Because that's how it was spitting." answered, Carmellette.

(Ellie said to herself) See, I hate this I'm always coming in at the end of what is going on.

"You did not see Sam do that!" Phyllis said in a stern voice.

"You right, he didn't, his penis did, right in the out house," replied Doris.

One of, Ellie's eyebrows went up.

"Take it back, that's disgusting - awful about a future political leader!" shouted Phyllis.

"No, thinking about him being a political leader is disgusting, not his penis spitting," said, Carmellette laughing along with Doris and Ellie.

"How dare you joke—laugh at Sam?" asked Phyllis.

"Easy," said Carmellette.

"Easy—you're right about easy. It's easy to walk away from a female who is not really a female and that is exactly what Ervin did. Walked or the town heard ranned away!" Phyllis then grinned.

"What are you talking about?" continued Doris. "Look at Carmellette, look at those titties, big ripe melons, look at her hips and her butt. They are carbon copies of waves of an ocean. A perfect female, the mothers of all seas birthed her and their arms carried her to shore. A mermaid that turned human and you're just jealous!" ended Doris.

"Just because something walks like a duck or quacks like a duck. May not necessarily be a duck." Then Phyllis stormed out and walked back into the living room to join the others chanting a biblical song.

"Another stupid parable," whispered Ellie.

"What?" asked Doris.

"Oh nothing—just talking to myself," said Ellie.

"Well don't answer yourself back or people might just think you're crazy?" replied Doris.

"Crazy, maybe that is what I should become to get understandable answers and not these stupid parables," continued Ellie. "The duck, the dogs and the catfish don't make any sense." Then Ellie stormed out too and joined the rest in the living room.

"Carmellette, what are you doing?" asked Doris.

"Do you think, I'm pregnant?" Carmellette said while rubbing her stomach.

"Did you and Ervin do anything?" asked Doris.

"What do you mean?" asked Carmellette.

"You know what I mean," sighed Doris.

"Virgin Mary didn't have to do anything," Answered Carmellete.

"Well that can't happen again," said Doris.

"Why not?" asked Carmellette.

"Because, she was white—pure," said Doris.

"Oh," sighed Carmellette.

"Oh, is right." sighed Doris.

Then those two joined the rest in the living room. While Pastor Caldwell was finally finishing up bless'en over the now cold food. *{He really think, he be doing something}*

"See, Jesus is Jesus. The father of Jesus is the father of Jesus and the Holy Ghost is the Holy Ghost. But they are considered as one. Example: On your body you have a head, ears, and arms; well accept for brother Louis he has one arm, praised the Lord.

But continue the stomach, legs and feet. It's still all on one body. Not three or four bodies but one body. Not on Mary's body or Joseph's body, but your body. Your body is unique. Those three spirits in heaven is one body. That is unique and Sister Henderick's pork chops are also unique. Can I get an amen?" said Pastor Caldwell.

The rest of the bible study people said, "Amen"

Then, Pastor Caldwell said, "Okay let's eat."

And we ate.

After bible study, Doris was still sitting down in a corner of the living room reading the Bible. Now listening about the Bible is one thing, but for Doris to read is another. "I don't see anything here about it," said Doris.

"About what?" Ellie asked.

"About machines," Doris answered back.

"Machines?" Ellie asked.

"Yes machines. Machines do what people want them to do and when their tired of that machine, they just throw it away." Doris started crying.

"I'm sorry, but you're not making any sense," replied Ellie.

"I am making sense. It's this so called Bible that's not making any sense. There are all kinds of people written in here that has been forgiven. The liars, the phonicators, thieves, those that preach false doctrine and other sinners. But nowhere is it in here about machines! When is God going to have a prophet to write about machines?" asked Doris.

"You're using machines as a metaphor. A metaphor to who?" Ellie wanted to know.

"To me," whispered Doris.

And for the first time, Ellie understood another factor about life from her grandmother.

That is *{you will always meet someone who has a deeper pain than you}*

What Kind Of Flower?

"Something is wrong with me," said Carmellette.

"Yes there is and we need to talk," replied Ellie.

"Observed me, what do you see?" asked Carmellette.

"I see a girl, a pretty girl, prettiest girl in town, a smart girl, the smartest girl in town. I see a girl who is before her time. I see a woman, no I take that back. The woman that folks will admire far away and close. I see what you see," said Ellie.

"Sleepless nights is what I also been seeing," said Carmellette.

"Why?" asked Ellie.

"A good question, a question that only, Ervin could answer if he was not dead. Stupid, just like Sam, a stupid little boy," said Carmellette.

"What happen that day?" asked, Ellie.

"Nothing, not a damn thing!" Carmellette said angrily.

"Something happen," said Ellie.

"I said nothing happen. He wouldn't take it. So something is wrong with me. Everybody knows but me. What is it?" asked Carmellette.

"You're to pushy and direct and that's what scares boys off, I guess," answered Ellie.

"I will be no doormat for no man," said Carmellette.

"If you don't change your ways, you want have a man," said Ellie.

"Then Joan of Arc, I will be!" shouted Carmellette.

"She was set on fire," said Ellie.

"By stupid men!" said Carmellete.

The next day

"Grandmother, what is wrong with, Carmellette?" Ellie asked her grandmother.

"Nothing, Ellie but there is something wrong with you. Your memory. Remember, I told you about a catfish. A male catfish can fertilize and reproduce. Now go on and play.

Then, grandmother Samford reached in the bucket for a catfish. Cut the head off and scaled it.

"Ellie" her grandmother shouted out for her.

"Yes-mam," Ellie came back in the kitchen.

"Carmellette is going to have to figure it out for herself, of who she is. And she is not alone. The Bible speaks of it. Those kinds of people. Nevertheless, you're a good friend, trying to help. But like I said, that is a road she has to travel alone. And a long road at that. And that road won't start until she leaves this little town. When she ventures out and sees the world as the world really is. She can handle herself. She sho' do got a mouth on her. My opinion she already knows what she is, but she is scared. In life you will find a lot of humans are scared of their own shadow. Until somebody make them look and look hard!"

My grandmother's words ended.

Persona

A persona image, I hold true to myself
more rooted than a hundred year old tree
more higher where raindrops form
more deeper (in memory of) Hitler's hate!

A persona image, I keep within
more vulnerable than a placenta
more secret than molestation to a child
more disease that don't, want to die!

A persona image, I the narrator of my life
more lips that lies (I hear)
more than deceiving eyes (I meet)
more hindering hugs (I still receive)

My persona
in my walk
in my talk
in my speech that teaches
perseverance make a perfect persona of thy self!

There are only two things that my, Grandmother Samford would go into her secret money jar for. One is a new fabric print that she seldom sees at the town general store and money to spend at the once a year carnival that comes to our small county.

But this year was different as my grandmother, aunt and myself walked up the steps a carnival sign hanging in the store window. With pictures and bold colorful words of the spectacular show coming soon. As we enter in the general store there was something else that caught my grandmother's eyes. A new fabric color.

But not just a standard fabric color, it was satin. A light brown satin color. She touched it, picked the bulk up and held it like a baby caressing it. And then she started waltzing around in the store with it. She was in her own world, one we did not know. But wherever she was, she was having a good time. For next she started singing softly in her native tongue. Finally, more embarrassment came. My Aunt Effie joined in the dance behind her. So now it look like three subjects were dancing. My Aunt Effie holding on to my grandmother shoulders from behind, my grandmother and this bulk of material just waltzing away and singing together. I'm glad that the general store keeper spoke up and said, "Ladies are we buying or crying?" commenting about their singing.

Aunt Effie and my grandmother, stopped waltzing and singing and looked around the store and saw the other customers faces laughing.

The storekeeper and I did not see anything funny. As a matter of fact, I was quite worried. They say that you're old once, but young twice. Maybe their brain cells have now started to slowly deteriorate? Who knows.

After those two composed themselves together again. They both walked up to the counter and my grandmother said, "Oh dear, I forgot my money." My Aunt Effie said, "that's okay" and right in front of the storekeeper's eyes she pulled up her blouse, flashed those big yellow double D's titties, reached in her bustanaire between her bosom, her tongue sticking out on the side of her mouth, she finally felt her money that was wraped in a small cloth and pulled it out and laid the tied up cloth on the counter. With her blouse still pulled up. The storekeeper gave an unpleasant stare. It most have been unpleasant, because my aunt's reaction was ugly. "What, you never seen damn titties before?" "Well if you haven't here is a better look!" Then she pulled out one of her yellow double D's titties, which almost touched the counter top. The storekeeper stepped back with his mouth wide open and said, "Please leave."

My Aunt Effie, put her tittie back in her bustanaire and fastened up her blouse and said to the store keeper, "You could have touched you damn scary cat!" And she walked out with my grandmother carrying the whole bulk of brown satin material out of the store and I right behind her. I think we just became thieves!

I Know God's Laughing Now

We were just about to go in the house from sitting out on the porch that evening. Aunt Effie, my grandparents and myself, when my grandpa said, "got company."

The rest of us looked out to the road as the car droved in front of the house. It was the white storekeeper; he got out, closed his car door and walked up to the porch. My Aunt Effie, was sitting on the porch banister, my grandparents on the porch swing and I standing at the door. "Good evening folks, sorry to trouble you at this late hour, but I tried to get here earlier. Got occupied and the time went ahead of me. Time can do that you know, when you're balancing the books. Yap, time is a selfish thing, don't wait on anybody. Like, I said, I would have come out here earlier, well really, I'm 3 days late with this."

He held out my Aunt Effie's cloth and money. Continuing he said, "It's all there, I'm mean your change and all. I took out the cost for the bulk of material. I gladly gave up a nice discount. Well here it is." And the storekeeper's arm reach further out toward my Aunt Effie. As her arm reached to take the cloth and change from his hand, my Grandpa Samford arm reached out and took it before my Aunt Effie could. My

Grandpa Samford said to the store keeper, "thank you and good night".

My Aunt Effie drew her arm back in. The store keeper, walked back to his car, but turned around and said, "Miss Effie would you have dinner with me?"

My Aunt Effie arch in her back straightens up to speak.

"No," said my Grandpa, then he spoke to us, "in the house ladies."

My grandmother knew my aunt did not want to go in the house, so she helped her with a little encouragement. "You're in this man's house," I heard her whisper to my aunt.

"But, I'm no damn child," my aunt whispered back.

"Okay then you can be a homeless grownup," said my grandmother to my aunt, smiling and whispering at the same time.

And with that in mind, my Aunt Effie was suddenly encouraged to go in the house.

Another lesson in life *{When you're against a wall, be careful that you don't become the wall for if you do, you will loose your identity}*

And that what was happening to my Aunt Effie, she started to become the walls of the house and was reminded of it. Just like the walls do not have any say so, she really did not have say so either.

We went in the house, but my grandpa stayed out. He re-lit his cigar, the third puff he spoke out to the storekeeper. "In Africa, they have biracial Africans people now, it's sad that nothing is really pure, genuine and it's going to get worse. Africa is going to be more populated with white people or governed more by white people."

The store keeper, closed his car door and came back around, he put his foot on the front of the bumper of his car and said, "I don't know about, Africa, Africans or their politics."

My grandpa drew on his cigar again and said, "then why do you want to date an African descendant?"

The store keeper finished tieing his shoestring, straightened up his pants legs and said, "Well hell, I didn't know that she was from, Africa. I thought she was Hispanic, Latin or something like that. She's beautiful."

My grandpa Samford took another deep puff on his cigar with the smoke still in his mouth and said, "African people or not?" Then slowly blew out the smoke.

The storekeeper, gave a slight laugh, moved his neck around and said, "I'm not here to fuss and fight, I'm here."

My grandpa interfered and said, "I know what you're here for and you're not going to get it. See, Sir no one here has a price tag on their head, only good morals have respected regards here. As long as I breathe in this house, it shall stay and continue so."

"But she's a grown woman!" The white storekeeper, pointed at the house.

"Then take her and give her-her own premises!" my grandpa shouted out.

"It's just a date not marriage!" the storekeeper shouted back.

"Leave my sight." said my grandpa, then my Grandpa reached under the porch swing, came up with his rifle and cocked it.

Then the storekeeper said, "she won't get another discount—rest assured on that." And with that he got in his car and left.

Oh, did I mention that my grandpa is biracial too. Cherokee, do I need to say more?

"I just can't believe that white man would come over here and the reasons behind it," said Ellie's Aunt Lucette.

Ellie sneaked in from outside through the kitchen way and kneeled down in the corner of the kitchen close to the living room. Hearing the grownups conversing. She knew growing up in this house that children should be seen and not heard and children don't need to be around grown folks when they're talking. Certain business a children shouldn't hear is what they teach and practice around here.

"Well he did, a man is a man. And I have had my share of men, they don't surprise me anymore. How they justify their reason for doing something or something that they had already done. I've been a fool to few to accept some of those reasons, just to have a man, just so I wouldn't be alone. And for what, when you think about it, you really are alone. Because he really don't want to be with you. He's waiting, like you're waiting. You're waiting for him to change and he's waiting for a better way out, if that change comes.

You look up and what you see, you and him, now old and still miserable people cursing about life. When a child is born it's already unhappy, that's why it cries, when it comes out of the mother's womb. Day one it's unsatisfied, hurt, confused and griping about what? It does not really know. Yet it cries to tell, give warnings and vent out. I WANT A CHANGE!" shouted Aunt Effie as she jumped to her feet.

"More tea?" said my grandma to Aunt Lucette.

"Thank you." replied Aunt Lucette.

"Sit down, Effie, you look lost," said my grandma.

"You making fun of me?" asked my Aunt Effie.

"It is not Christian to make fun of hurt," said my grandma.

"Then what are you doing?" asked my Aunt Effie.

"I'm doing a sisterly duty, I need for you to sit down so that I can talk to you. You're making me dizzy," said my Grandma Ivory.

"I don't want to hear no preach'en today," sighed my Aunt Effie as she sat down.

"Two words that's all," said my Grandma.

"Okay what are they?" asked my Aunt Effie.

"**Move – On,**" said my Grandma

"I have moved on, I'm here," replied my Aunt Effie.

"Yes you are, but not your mind and it's slowly killing you. You are not the only one that has had a broken heart. A heart that was just as fragile and valuable as a porcelain plate. You are not the only one, that has told themselves. If I stay, I'm unhappy and if I go, I still might be unhappy. You are not the only one that life has lied to. Look at me, my best friend married my fiancé. Look at Lucette, years of frustrations with this man. Give it to the Lord the preacher said every Sunday and Lucette's husband still left her.

And, God please spare my precious granddaughter from a broken heart, I pray every night. They say that God hears all prayers, but I've been convinced in my life that he dose not hear stupid ones. That's why things don't change the way you want them to change. That's why you work hard at something that should not be so. But you want it, you feel you need it, you think it needs you. Complications come back and forth. You asked yourself why? When you know the reason, but you're the fruit that want to be admired in every season. Like watermelon," ended my grandma.

"Honey speaking of watermelon, Ivory do you remember the time, when we ate so much watermelon that one summer? My stomach started cramping and I felt wetness in my bloomers. So, I went to the outhouse and was scared of what I seen. I shouted out and said *{Ivory, I'm peeing watermelon color!}* when really I started on my cycle."

Now laughing, Aunt Lucette who was really trying to break up the fog drama feeling of her two sisters' conversation. But, it didn't work.

Aunt Effie stood up again and started talking.

"I could never move mentally, not after what he did to me. I wish I would have known that he went two ways. I walked in and caught them in our bed. He had a woman on the left and a woman on the right. Damn, he was a freaky Bast_rd! Now how in the hell, I supposed to compete with that?"

The two other sisters' expression showed agreement.

Another lesson I was taught. *{No matter how a woman put out. Sexually, financially or become co-dependant for him. There is always somebody better than her and a man is just like a dog, leashed or not leashed, if it comes closer, he's going to do more than sniff}*

I Humble *At Your Honesty*

Beautiful you say I am
talentive you speak of me
an irregular attitude you told one's about me

(laughing) I humble at your honesty

Yet you constantly reaching for me
desire of making love to me again

The moment comes

And before those ecstacy sheets become clean and fold, you
suffer with rage behind my name...because you made me to
believe that you had suddenly put up a dead end sign
around/in/about our relationship

Those same soft sexy lips of yours the sound of your voice
can now shattered all window panes in a big catholic
church...those horrible words that come out, I not weep but.

(laughing) I humble at your honesty

The moon sleeps, the sun wakes, the stars blink, the weather
withers, age comes and death goes

Yet you constantly reaching for me
seeking comfort from the person (i) who caused you the most
pain
re-kindling memories of our mating now stands before us

You already know my reaction

And that's why

(laughing) I humble at your honesty

11 Letters Each—Nervousness & Selfishness

Some people are nervous on their wedding day, nervous on their first day on the job or at a new school, nervous having to speak or sing in front of an audience, nervous in meeting your future in-laws, nervous in seeing an old acquaintance, nervous to take on a task that you think you're going to fail at or just nervous meeting someone for the first time, the one that seeded you or birthed you, nervous if stopped or approached by a law officer, nervous on getting a new look, nervous or anticipating on something you already now it exists, nervous about getting or going to heaven especially when they have done nothing but wrong renaming themselves equinoxes on the planet that we call earth!

My mother, Ruth is an equinox spirit. I was told night and day is always the same for her. I'm not going to save you from all the dull dialogue that was said that day.

For if I would have taken the longer route home, with my friends again. I would have missed her. She's in my room, touching my things, why?

Ellie said to herself as she watched her mother, Ruth, from the doorway entrance.

Ruth noticing Ellie in the doorway said, "the last time, I was here, over there in that corner was a baby bed, for you. The big bed was over there, there was a different dresser, the room color has changed, but I like it."

This is my first time hearing her speak, with understanding. First time looking at her, with interest eyes. I've seen pictures, but people change in pictures. Ellie thought to herself.

My mother broke the silence again "Can't believe this used to be my room."

"Do you want it back?" I asked.

"Oh no, it's yours." my mother said.

"How long are you staying?" I asked my mother.

"Oh, I'm about to go, my ride can't stay long," she said.

"I don't know why, but I picture you a little smaller," I said.

"Well, you know, life is good and my friend he loves lots of extra cushion," she replied.

"That's nice," I said.

"Well, I just wanted to see my old room and you take care," Ruth said as she passed by me, her blood, her daughter, her future help if she's bless with old age. No comfort of touch.

Years have passed the distance not of my fault but hers. How does she do it, pacify her pitiful reasons?

I watch her go downstairs Grandma handed Ruth an envelope, and handed the man, my mama's friend, a basket of food. They walked out the house and before my mama got in the car she turned around and said to my grandma "Mama, I'll pay you back one day." And those two drove off.

When will I see her again? Ellie asked the question to herself and answered it.

Right now, how I feel at this very moment; I can function with out that favor from God!

<u>**Hidden Blessing**</u>

I was knocked in the head and recovered some common sense
A painful hidden blessing

I was kicked and punched
I was lied to
I was left alone
I was defeated and never knew that I was in a game

I was buried
I was suffocated
I died
mentally

I did not know
I did not know
the score
and the cheating opponents
were not sure themselves

Yet
I always try my best to play fair
for a respectful player gets more attention
and monuments are built in their honor

Losing is a hard pill to swallow
God wants everybody in heaven

But
Satan is better where he is
and for that, that is also a

Hidden Blessing

The Alpha, But Not The Omega

"Carmellette, you wanna sleep over, Saturday night?" asked Ellie.

"Yeah, why not," replied Carmellette.

"Okay see you then," said Ellie.

Later on that evening Carmellette arrived. "Ellie your guest is here—Carmellette," hollered Aunt Effie toward upstairs.

"Tell her to come upstairs, please," ellie shouted back down.

Carmellette, walked upstairs to Ellie's room. "Hey."

"Hey back," said Ellie.

"Thanks for inviting me. Anytime that I can get away from my family is great," replied Carmellette.

"Yeah, I know what you mean. One day I'll be leaving to visit my mother. She was not financially able to let me go back with her. So, I'm going to start saving up my own train fare and spending money. She will be so proud of me," said, Ellie.

"Do your grandmother know about your plans?" asked Carmellette.

"No and don't you tell her. Repeat after me. *{Stick a needle in my eye if I do}* and then spit in my hands and let's shake on it," said Ellie.

"Saying that is fine, but how are you going to trust my handshake? Remember, I'm going to be a politician," said Carmellette.

The two girls started laughing.

"Do you really want to go into law?" asked Ellie

"Does a cat meow?" responded Carmellette.

"Have you ever heard of a dog, Meow?" Ellie asked another question.

"It depends on what planet you're from!" replied Carmellette.

"Girl, you're so silly. Yeah, you should go into politics. You'll have the jury and other listeners confused and baffled," said Ellie.

"Thank you, all in a days work of a politician's lifestyle," said Carmellette.

"Speaking of lifestyles, what kind do you really wanna have?" asked Ellie.

"I'm not following you," said Carmellette.

Are you going to flaunt your female qualities to the top or are you going to bogart every man you see just to get to the top?" asked Ellie.

"Showing my stockings is unprofessional. My sincere voice will tell them where, I stand," said Carmellette.

"But your sincere voice scares people off, especially men," replied Ellie.

"I'm not going to change, they will eventually accept me as I am. I will be a good asset in the world of government. One day they will see my actions and be very impressed. For example, Ervin, who has been found dead; if I had the case I would have been found his killer or his killers. Right now, I can't do anything about it, but this town will see a trial someday. Sad to say, that this town would go on and start living their lives again and forget this unforsaken mishap. But my soul will keep the flames about seeking honesty behind Ervin's death inside of me. I have a funny feeling that these killers are hiding their secret in the church!

Matthew 7. VS. 22-23

"Where is he again?" said Phyllis.

"Down by the tree," Sam pointed.

"Let's go!" Phyllis takes a step toward the tree.

"No way, I'm not going down there" said Sam.

"I said let's go!" tugging on Sam's shirt.

"Oh God," cried out Sam.

"Shut up!" said Phyllis.

"He's Dead, he's really dead, oh Jesus, you know that I didn't mean to do it. It was an accident." Sam started reciting Psalms 32 verse 1-4 over and over again out loud.

"Blessed is he whose transgression is forgiven, whose sin is covered.

Blessed is the man unto whom the Lord imputeth not iniquity, and in whose spirit there is no guile. When I kept silence, my bones waxed old through my roaring all the daylong. For day and night thy hand was heavy upon me: my moisture is turned into the drought of summer. Selah."

He noticed Phyllis rip the back of the shirt on the dead body in half.

"What are you doing?" asked Sam.

"Covering our tracks," answered Phyllis.

"Our tracks?" Sam replied puzzled.

"Yes you got us in this mess," said Phyllis.

"Don't do that!" He bent down to grab Phyllis by one of her wrists.

"Why not? He's a dead nigger!" said Phyllis as she snatched her wrist back and continued what she was doing.

Sam then noticed Phyllis taking a small sharp object from between her bible pages. The sharp object is not what stunned him it is what she did with it. She took the sharp object and slightly carved the initials of KKK on the back of the dead body.

"There she said, you can see it, but it's not bleeding. The initials look old by us doing it that way," Phyllis said.

"You're crazier than he was—you have lost your mind!" Sam said as he stepped back.

"I love you," Phyllis said as she reached out for Sam.

Sam stepped back further.

"Our future Sam," Phyllis continued.

"What future?" said Sam.

"Your political future, I'm your partner, our happiness. Don't spoil this. It doesn't make any sense to have two dead niggers, because that is exactly what's going to happen if the law finds out the truth," said Phyllis.

"But it was an accident!" Sam said, as he looked to the heavens.

"Then go and tell them the truth and see what happens. But let me save you a trip, I'll tell you what's going to happen." Phyllis, grabbed Sam's chin making Sam look at her as she continued. "Accident or no accident, you will be in jail until you're a dead nigger. So go on, go and tell the white man the truth!" Phyllis' finger pointed up to the dirt road. Sam looked up at the dirt road. Was it an accident or was he lying to himself?

Now looking at Ervin's once upon a time body of life when spirits used to dance through it. Now just laying there like a broken clay pot. No use to anybody now.

Ervin should not have disrespected Sam that day when their paths crossed. Ervin did not speak, Sam thinking to himself now. That day is all coming back. He remembered how Ervin's mind was occupied on something or was he talking to himself. A strange boy, a crazy boy and rudely. Even though he did not care for Ervin's friendship, he still spoke to him when he saw him that day. But Ervin didn't speak back and that is what made him mad. So mad, that he remembered grabbing Ervin by the shirt…and how he became a monster after that.

"Why?" He said to himself. Why did the girls like Ervin more than him? "He was stupid", the girls said, "but he's cute even though." Church members prayed for him every Sunday for Ervin to change. Well that change has come, he's dead!

"I don't know where you are my love," Phyllis clapping in Sam's face then she continued talking. "This is how we found him you understand me?" she said to Sam.

Sam just shook his head up and down.

"Good, okay now take his shirt completely off, shake it off, and hand it to me," ordered Phyllis for Sam to do.

Sam with one eye closed, took the shirt completely off the dead body. Shook it off and handed to Phyllis like she instructed him to do. Sam almost fainted doing this horrible task.

Phyllis then took the shirt and finished ripping it in half. Then she took the shirt and rips it some more. Next she stuffs some of the rip shirt in her left bra and the rest in her right bra.

"Okay, how do I look now?" She asked Sam.

"Yeah," Sam answered nonchantly with one of his eyes still closed.

"Listen, I hear a car coming." Phyllis ran to the dirt road and then flagged the car to stop.

It was Pastor Caldwell. Phyllis walked up to the car on the driver side.

Pastor Caldwell eyes bucked out with amazement and said, "Girl you have really blossom, look at the Lord working." Then he blew out a long whistle.

"Yes Sir, he's a mighty good God, but not for that boy down there," Phyllis said.

"What boy?" asked Pastor Caldwell.

Phyllis pointed down the hill. "We think it's Ervin, but we're children we don't know for sure," said Phyllis.

"Of course not. You didn't touched nothing did you?" Asked Pastor Caldwell.

"No, no, I'm to scared, look at my hands shaking," said Phyllis.

"You precious thing," said Pastor Caldwell.

"I don't know if I can hold the collection plate stable tomorrow at church" Phyllis then looked sad after she spoke.

"Well will make sure you sit out, where you ushers usually sit. We do not want no money spilling out of the collection plate, which would be the invisible hands of Satan." He spoke while getting out of his car and he continued speaking. "Now let's go and see the body," Pastor Caldwell ended.

"Oh Lord," said Phyllis.

"What's wrong?" asked Pastor Caldwell.

"The spirit touched me, I felt a kiss from the Holy Ghost," said Phyllis.

"A shamma mama rock!" shouted Pastor Caldwell and raised his arms in the air.

"Pastor Caldwell, down there is Sam with that corpse. I can't see it again. Nightmares fallen upon me now as we speak of it," Phyllis said.

"Then it's best that you stay up here," said Pastor Caldwell.

"Brace yourself," said Phyllis.

"I'm okay, praying over dead bodies are my best sermons," replied Pastor Caldwell.

"Even those with initials?" asked Phyllis.

"What initials?" said Pastor Caldwell.

"KKK," whispered Phyllis.

Pastor Caldwell, slightly chuckled for he didn't know what else to do, his feelings were unsure. Hatred in their town? No. Probably on an eclipsed moon it might be a one on one personal confrontation between two parties. Not a group thing. Not a racial thing. Not in their town. Nevertheless, he still had to go down there and see for himself.

Phyllis pointed toward the direction of the dead body. Pastor Caldwell slowly walked down to the murder sight. He saw Sam standing by the dead body. One of Sam's eyes was still shut closed. That was strange Pastor Caldwell thought as he now looked over the dead body and shook his head with grief. But Sam knew why one of his eyes was shut completely closed. That was a punishment from God, because Sam only told half the truth. He would forever see half of the world.

I Can't Give You Tomorrow

The promise of love you were hoping for

The apology you're asking

The truth that was took from a love poem verse.

I can't give you tomorrow

A magic portion to hide and sealed those scars, I allowed upon you

A prayer that been played out, reciting will no longer leave my lips

A kiss, the last kiss I secretly hold within, in my heart and spirit.

I can't give you tomorrow

Our loving laughter together again

Our future that was faked…so see I can't give you tomorrow

For tomorrow will tell my life of lies.

The End